MATT CHRISTOPHER

On the Field with...

Emmitt Smith

1837

Little, Brown and Company

Boston   New York   Toronto   London

First Edition

Library of Congress Cataloging-in-Publication Data
Christopher, Matt.
  On the field with — Emmitt Smith / Matt Christopher. — 1st ed.
      p.   cm.
  ISBN 0-316-13722-7
  1. Smith, Emmitt. — Juvenile literature.   2. Football
players — United States — Biography — Juvenile literature.   3. Dallas
Cowboys (Football team) — History.   I. Title.
GV939.S635C47   1997
796.332′092 — dc21
[B]   97-12530

                    10   9   8   7   6   5   4
                         COM-MO

Published simultaneously in Canada by Little, Brown & Company
(Canada) Limited

Cover photograph by Robert Rogers/Sports Illustrated © Time Inc.

Printed in the United States of America

Contents

Chapter One:
1969-83

Mighty Mini-Mite

One evening when Emmitt Smith III was a baby, his father, Emmitt Jr., and his mother, Mary, were relaxing in the living room of the family home. Suddenly, they heard a loud *thump* in the next room.

They looked at each other, then jumped to their feet. The noise had come from young Emmitt's room, where he was taking a nap in his crib. His parents were worried that something awful had happened.

As they raced toward the door, Emmitt Smith III came toddling through the doorway, a triumphant little smile on his face. He was only nine months old but had already learned how to climb out of his crib and walk. Not many nine-month-old babies can even walk.

But that's Emmitt Smith for you. He has always

1

done what others have thought was impossible. In fact, he has made a career out of it.

From the time he was a young boy, Emmitt wanted to play pro football for the Dallas Cowboys. By focusing on his goal and working hard, Emmitt kept improving and finally achieved his dream.

At nearly every stage of Emmitt's football career, someone always questioned whether he could succeed at the next level. People were always saying he was too short, too slow, or too something to keep playing well.

That never stopped Emmitt. He simply remained focused on his goal. And each time he reached a goal, he would set his sights on another one. When he began playing football in high school, his first goal was to make the starting lineup. He did, and so he set new goals — eventually becoming one of the best high school running backs in history and earning a college scholarship.

The same strategy served Emmitt well at the University of Florida. He began his career on the bench but soon became a Heisman Trophy candidate and one of the best running backs in college football. When he joined the Dallas Cowboys of the National

Football League, he continued to set goals for himself. Now he is the best running back in pro football and one of the greatest football players of all time!

When Emmitt was a baby, his parents thought he might become a football player. Only a few days after he started walking, he started running! Each time his parents came toward him with their arms outstretched, Emmitt just laughed and ran away. Even then, he was hard to catch.

He loved football from the moment he first set eyes on the game. Before Emmitt celebrated his first birthday, his mother noticed that the only time he seemed to settle down and stay quiet was when there was a football game on television. So every time a game came on, she placed Emmitt in a windup swing in front of the TV. Emmitt would stare at the screen for hours, enthralled, as if he were studying each play.

"I remember it before anything else," Emmitt once told a reporter, "sitting there watching, wanting to play. It's my earliest memory. Before anything else, there was football."

The game of football has always been important to

the Smith family. Emmitt's father was a star defensive back at Washington High School in Pensacola, Florida, a city of about 60,000 in the Florida panhandle. He received some interest from a few big-time colleges that wanted to offer him a scholarship to play football.

But Emmitt Jr. injured his knees in high school. The scholarships never materialized, so instead of enrolling in a large four-year school, he attended a two-year junior college.

But in his very first season, his mother, Erma Lee, became ill and had to be confined to a wheelchair. His father, Emmitt Sr., already worked long and hard as a laborer at a factory. He needed someone to help take care of Erma Lee.

Emmitt Jr. volunteered. As Erma Lee's only child, he knew she needed him. Although athletics were important to him, his family was even more important. He set aside his dream of attending college and playing sports. He quit school and took a job as a bus driver for the city of Pensacola. Emmitt Sr. and Emmitt Jr. arranged to work different shifts so someone was always at home with Erma Lee.

A few years later, Emmitt Jr. married. He and his

wife, Mary, settled in a small house in a housing project only a few blocks away from his parents.

The young couple soon had a daughter, Marsha. Then, on May 15, 1969, they had a little boy they named Emmitt III, after his father and grandfather. The Smiths later had three more children, all boys: Erik, Emory, and Emil.

The Smiths weren't rich, but Emmitt's father worked hard to support the family. Although they didn't have a lot of possessions, there was plenty of love to go around.

As the oldest of four brothers, Emmitt had many playmates. The four brothers got together with their cousins almost every day to ride bikes and play in nearby parks. One of Emmitt's favorite games was football.

Mary Smith didn't mind that her boys enjoyed playing outside, but she didn't care for the dirty pants and shirts they came home in after playing football. So after the boys left home to play, they would take off their pants and shirts, turn them inside out, and put them back on to play. Then, before they returned home, they would turn their clothes right side out again so all the dirt was on the inside. That way, they thought, their mother wouldn't know they had been playing football.

Mary soon figured out their ruse, but she didn't make Emmitt or his brothers stop playing football. She knew the game was their favorite sport.

Every time an NFL game was on television, Emmitt dropped everything to watch. The Dallas Cowboys were his favorite team. His favorite players were Cowboy quarterback Roger Staubach and running back Tony Dorsett. When Emmitt played football on the sandlots, he usually pretended he was one of those two players.

When Emmitt was eight years old, his family moved from the projects into their own home a few blocks away. His grandparents lived right next door.

He loved being close to his grandmother and grandfather. Sometimes, Emmitt even stayed overnight to help take care of Erma Lee. Although she couldn't walk, she set a good example for Emmitt, who remembers that "she was the strongest person I knew." Despite her illness, she was never sad or pessimistic. Instead, she had a smile for everyone and always encouraged Emmitt to do his best.

He usually did. Emmitt's mother made sure all her children studied hard and went to church every Sunday morning. Emmitt enjoyed the singing that took place at every service, but when the minister started giving his sermon, Emmitt and his brothers sometimes became antsy and started acting up. The only way Mary could keep them in line was to whisper, "If you boys behave, you can all play football when we get home." That was usually enough to ensure the boys' good behavior.

In 1975, Emmitt became eligible to play organized football in the local Mini-Mite league. Emmitt's father wasn't eager for him to play. His own old football injuries made him worry for his son. He didn't want Emmitt to get hurt.

But Emmitt wanted to play football more than anything else in the world. He pestered his mother every day to let him play. Mary Smith knew how much it meant to him and finally convinced her husband to allow their son to play. Emmitt was thrilled.

He joined a team sponsored by the Salvation Army. In his first season, Emmitt played quarterback.

The team was successful, and Emmitt was the star. He passed or ran the ball nearly every play. He was more mature than most of the other boys, which gave him a big advantage.

But some of Emmitt's opponents thought his team was trying to cheat. They accused Emmitt of being older and bigger than the league rules allowed. The league matched players of similar weight and size so that no one would be at a disadvantage. As a player grew larger, he would move up to a league with bigger boys. They asked to weigh him and see his birth certificate before almost every game.

That didn't bother Emmitt. It just made him more determined.

On the first day of practice in his second year, Emmitt's coach told him, "You're not playing quarterback this season."

"Wh-what?" sputtered Emmitt. He was crestfallen. He loved playing quarterback.

"This season," said his coach, "we're gonna toss you the football and let you run. You're a running back."

At first, Emmitt was disappointed. But he soon discovered that he liked being a running back. In fact, it felt as if he already knew how to play the position. Although Emmitt was big and fast, it was

good team. In fact, they were terrible. It had been twenty-one seasons since they had had a winning record. The past four seasons they had won only three games and lost twenty-seven. But Emmitt didn't care. He just wanted to play.

That spring, Escambia hired a new coach, Dwight Thomas. Thomas had been fired from a bigger high school despite compiling a stellar 30–12 record the previous four seasons. The school principal had told him, "We need to win the state championship, and to do that, we need a coach who has already won one."

Being fired like that angered Thomas. He thought his record had been good enough for him to keep his job. Coach Thomas decided he had something to prove. He told that school principal, "I'm going to find the worst team in the state and come back and beat you."

Thomas didn't have to look very hard to find the worst team. The only open coaching job was at lowly Escambia. He jumped at the opportunity to coach there, convinced he could turn one of the worst football programs in the state into one of the best.

Thomas made the rounds of all the local middle schools that spring and introduced himself to prospective players. Although he had heard about a certain running back named Emmitt Smith, Thomas had yet to meet him.

One day Thomas visited Brownsville and met with everyone interested in playing football. Most of the boys at the meeting were fooling around. But one boy stepped from the crowd, walked right up to Thomas, and stuck out his hand.

"Hello, Coach," the boy said. "I'm Emmitt."

Thomas was impressed. This wasn't a kid, he thought. This was a young man. He was polite, dressed well, and oozed self-confidence. He behaved more like an adult than a thirteen-year-old boy. Eighth-grade boys aren't supposed to act like this, thought Thomas.

He had just met Emmitt Smith.

Chapter Two:
1983–87

Setting Goals

Football for the Escambia High School varsity team began late the following summer. More than one hundred boys, including thirty-eight seniors, turned out for the first practice.

Emmitt and many of the younger players worried that with so many seniors around, they wouldn't get a chance to play. But from the very first day, Coach Thomas made it clear that this year, things would be different. There was no room on his team for players who weren't willing to follow instructions, do their best, and stay out of trouble.

"I have only three rules," Thomas told the boys before their first practice. "Be where you're supposed to be. Be there when you're supposed to be there. And be doing what you're supposed to be doing." Those rules, he said, pertained to more than football. He expected the team to follow them in school as well. If a player broke any of the rules, even once, Coach Thomas kicked him off the team.

Some of the upperclassmen snickered and smiled when Thomas spoke. But Emmitt knew the coach was serious. He didn't mind. His parents had already taught him how to behave. Emmitt knew he would have little trouble adhering to Coach Thomas's rules.

It wasn't long before some Gators learned just how serious Thomas was. They weren't used to being responsible for their own behavior. Almost every day, someone got kicked off the team for violating the rules. Many of the older players just plain quit.

That gave Emmitt and some of the younger players the only opportunity they needed. They believed in Coach Thomas and, once they got a chance to play, started believing in themselves.

One day just before the season, Coach Thomas addressed his team after practice. He talked about what he hoped to accomplish that season. Despite the fact that Escambia High hadn't had a winning season in more than two decades, he thought the team could win its league championship.

"It's a dream until you write it down," he told them. "Then it's a goal."

Those words made an impression on Emmitt. Ever since that day, Emmitt has made it a practice to set goals for himself. Before nearly every game, he writes down what he hopes to accomplish.

Before the first game, Emmitt achieved one of his goals. Coach Thomas switched the team's veteran tailback, Sam Bettis, to fullback to make room for Emmitt in the starting backfield.

In Coach Thomas's entire coaching career, only a handful of freshmen had ever made his team. None had ever made the starting lineup. But Thomas could tell that Emmitt was different.

He proved it in his first game. Facing Pensacola Catholic High School, Emmitt, one of the youngest players on the field, rushed for two touchdowns and 115 yards. Escambia won!

That fall, the talk around the table at the Smith house was all football. Emmitt's father had decided to show his sons that he still knew how to play the game. Despite his bad knees, he joined a semi-pro football team, the Pensacola Wings of the Dixie League, playing defensive back and wide receiver.

And Emmitt's little brother Emory was starring in youth league ball, following in Emmitt's footsteps by playing running back. Emmitt played on Friday nights, Emory played on Saturday mornings, and Emmitt Jr. played Saturday nights.

The Escambia High Gators were much improved. Although they still had an occasional poor game, such as a 51–0 loss to crosstown rival Pensacola High, they finished the season with a record of 7–3.

Emmitt was the big reason for the turnaround. For the season, he rushed the ball 256 times for 1,525 yards — an average of 5.9 yards per carry — and scored 19 touchdowns. And he was only fifteen years old!

When the football season ended, Emmitt went out for the basketball team. Although he stood only five foot nine, Emmitt could already dunk the ball. He tried out for the team and made the varsity.

But during football season, Emmitt had started lifting weights to increase his strength. When he returned to the basketball court, he discovered that his new muscles didn't respond the same way anymore. He simply couldn't hit a jump shot.

After being a star in middle school, Emmitt was

just another player on the varsity. He rarely played, eventually quitting to concentrate on football. Yet Emmitt still wanted to help the team.

He became a team manager, one of the guys who passes out towels to players during timeouts, makes sure everyone has enough water, and helps take care of the uniforms and equipment.

He didn't care that he was a big football star. He just wanted to help.

High school football is a big deal in the state of Florida. Teams hold practice sessions for upperclassmen in the spring and then begin again in earnest in late summer to prepare for the upcoming season. Because of the fine weather and strong competition, some of the best high school football players in the country come from Florida. College football coaches from across the nation go there to recruit players.

By the summer of 1984, Emmitt's sophomore season, he started receiving letters from colleges interested in having him attend and play football. Although most were just form letters like those mailed to hundreds of high school players, Emmitt began to realize that playing football could help him get into college.

Emmitt Smith had been a big surprise in the 1983 season, but now Escambia's opponents knew all about him. Football wasn't just for fun anymore. His team depended on him. Every time he stepped onto the field, he knew his performance could result in a college scholarship offer.

Emmitt was much improved in 1984. Lifting weights had made him stronger and quicker, but he started to realize that running the football required more than speed and strength. He began to run more intelligently, making use of his keen sight and sense of anticipation. He tried to fake out the defense and follow his blockers instead of just trying to outrun or run over players.

Now each time Emmitt touched the ball, he ate up huge chunks of yardage. Escambia started winning big.

Emmitt carried the ball nearly 30 times a game. By midseason, the pace started to wear on him.

He sprained both ankles. Emmitt wanted to keep playing, but his coaches didn't want him to risk further injury. So they compromised. Before facing Tallahassee's Rickard High, Emmitt had his ankles heavily taped. He still suited up, but his backup,

Gerald Williams, started the game. Emmitt would play only in an emergency.

He watched from the sidelines for most of the game. Late in the fourth quarter, Escambia trailed by a touchdown.

The emergency had happened. Coach Thomas looked over at Emmitt. Emmitt looked up at Coach Thomas. The two nodded at each other, and Emmitt ran onto the field as the crowd cheered.

Escambia had the ball on its own 11-yard line. The Gators were 89 long yards away from a touchdown.

Escambia started giving the ball to Emmitt. Sore ankles or not, he was determined to lead the team to a win.

Rickard couldn't stop him. He faked and followed his blocks as long as possible. If there was a player to run around, Emmitt ran around him. If there was a player to run over, Emmitt ran over him. He did whatever he had to do to keep moving downfield.

With only seconds left to play, Emmitt plunged into the end zone. On the 89-yard drive, he had gained 85 yards!

The score put the game into overtime. Emmitt stayed in.

Escambia got the ball and expertly marched down the field. As they neared the Rickard goal line, they put the ball into Emmitt's hands one more time.

He swept around end, eyeing the goal line. Then he angled upfield and was hit from the side as he left his feet to dive into the end zone.

Emmitt crossed the goal line, but it didn't matter. He had fumbled the ball! Rickard recovered.

Emmitt felt terrible. He was afraid that his mistake had cost Escambia the game. In the span of just a few moments, he had gone from being the hero to being the goat.

Fortunately, the Gators stopped Rickard cold, and Escambia won in overtime on a field goal. The fumble hadn't mattered.

But all of a sudden, Emmitt couldn't seem to hang on to the football. In one practice, he fumbled four or five times.

Escambia assistant coach Jim Nichols, who coached the offense, decided it was time to let Emmitt know how important it was to hold on to the football. It didn't matter that he was a big star. Nichols knew he had to treat Emmitt just like the other players.

First, he got in Emmitt's face. Then he let him have it.

"This isn't youth league ball anymore," blasted Nichols. "You will not be a great running back for this team or any team if you keep fumbling the football!"

Then Nichols made Emmitt take part in a grueling set of fumble drills. Over and over again, Nichols would toss the football to the ground. Emmitt would have to dive to the ground, wrap his arms around the ball, then spring to his feet and pitch the ball back to Nichols, who was already throwing another ball at Emmitt's feet. In only a few minutes, Emmitt was exhausted.

He learned his lesson. Over the next three seasons, he fumbled only five times.

Escambia cruised through the remainder of the season, losing only twice. The team qualified for the state playoffs in Division 3-A, the second-highest division in the state.

With Emmitt leading the way, Escambia rolled over its two postseason opponents, Bartow and Saint Petersburg, to capture the state championship. Emmitt ran for more than 200 yards in each game. In only two seasons, Escambia had gone from being the worst team in the state to being state champs!

Emmitt's statistics for his sophomore season were almost beyond belief. He gained 2,424 yards, with an average of 8.2 yards per carry. He wasn't just the best running back in the state of Florida, he was beginning to gain a national reputation. But some critics griped that most of Emmitt's yardage came against schools much smaller than Escambia. While they admitted that he was good, they didn't think he was *that* good.

In his junior year, Emmitt set out to prove his critics wrong. Because of increasing enrollment, the school moved up to Division 4-A, the group containing the biggest schools in Florida. Now no one could complain about the competition.

In the first game of the season, Escambia opened against Woodham High, the defending Division 4-A champions. Emmitt and the Gators would have to prove they belonged in the top division.

They did. Emmitt rolled for 236 yards despite being forced from the game late in the fourth quarter with a hip injury. Escambia kicker Alan Ward nailed a 50-yard field goal in the game's last minute to give Escambia a two-point win.

The victory set the tone for the remainder of the season. Most opponents got only a brief glimpse of Emmitt as he dashed by, the orange number 24 on his dark blue jersey growing smaller as he rumbled toward the end zone. Often, Emmitt played less than half the game, because Coach Thomas or Coach Nichols removed him if Escambia was way ahead. Emmitt raced for more than 200 yards in seven consecutive games, including a career-best 301 yards against Milton High.

In one game, Nichols pulled Emmitt early in the third quarter when Escambia's lead stretched to more than six touchdowns. After the game, the coach of the opposing team came bounding across the field toward Nichols, an angry look on his face.

Uh-oh, thought Nichols. He's going to complain about us running up the score. Doesn't he know that's why I pulled Emmitt?

As the other coach approached, Nichols braced himself for a tongue-lashing.

"Jimmy," yelled the coach. "What are you doing taking Emmitt out?"

"I-I have n-no intention of embarrassing you and your kids," explained Nichols.

The other coach just shook his head and started laughing. "Come on," he said, "I just like watching that kid run!"

Escambia made it to the Division 4-A championship game against Bradenton Southeast High School. For the second year in a row, Escambia made it look easy. Emmitt ran for 159 yards, and the Gators captured the state championship.

Once again, Emmitt's statistics were simply amazing. He scored an incredible 33 touchdowns and gained 2,918 yards on 353 carries. With one season remaining in his high school career, he was already among the greatest high school running backs of all time.

Emmitt was now famous. It seemed that every college in the country had contacted him, trying to convince him to attend their school. Meanwhile, national publications like *USA Today* and *Sports Illustrated* sent reporters to Pensacola to write stories about the most phenomenal running back in the country.

It would have been easy for Emmitt to get a big head, but his family wouldn't let him. His grandfather would sometimes take him to the bank where his mother worked, point out Mary Smith, and lecture Emmitt about the importance of hard work.

Those lessons took hold. Despite his growing fame, Emmitt still held a part-time job, first at a discount store, then at a local television station. He was still just a high school student.

But what a student! At the beginning of the season, Escambia was ranked by *USA Today* as the number one high school team in the country. Emmitt was on almost everybody's list as the nation's best prep running back.

Escambia's approach to the 1986 season was best summed up by Coach Thomas. "We do three things here on offense," he told a reporter. "We hand the ball to Emmitt, we pitch the ball to Emmitt, and we throw the ball to Emmitt."

For seven games, that was enough, as Emmitt and Escambia met all expectations. Escambia went undefeated and Emmitt was unstoppable. Then they faced their biggest rival, Pensacola High. Both teams needed a win to guarantee them a spot in the playoffs.

Emmitt and Escambia took control in the first half. He raced for more than 100 yards, and the Gators took a 10–3 lead.

A few minutes into the third quarter, Escambia had the ball on its own 49-yard line with fourth down and one yard to go. Emmitt got the ball.

As he took the handoff, Emmitt already knew that although he was supposed to run over right tackle, the hole would be closed. He saw the Pensacola defense all bunched up on the right side.

Emmitt didn't hesitate. Instead of charging off tackle, he changed direction and scooted outside a split second ahead of the defense.

He knew that all he had to do was turn the corner and he'd be gone. He raced to the sidelines just out of the reach of several defenders, then abruptly cut upfield.

The defenders dove at his feet. All they grasped was air.

Emmitt streaked down the sidelines for a touchdown. Escambia now led by two touchdowns!

But wait! As Emmitt charged into the end zone, instead of seeing the referee raise his hands over his head to signal six points, he saw the official waving his hands in front of his face and blowing his whistle. The play was dead!

Emmitt turned and looked around. At midfield, he saw an official pointing to the ground. Emmitt had stepped out of bounds when he turned the corner.

At least, that's what the official thought. Films of the game later proved that he was wrong. By then, it was too late.

The outcome of the game turned on that play. Pensacola took control and marched to two quick scores. Then Escambia panicked. Instead of giving the ball to Emmitt, it tried to pass. Emmitt ran the ball only once more the entire game. Escambia lost, 17–10.

They finished the season with a 10–1 record but weren't selected for the state playoffs.

Emmitt ran for "only" 1,937 yards, averaging 8.6 yards per attempt, on 225 carries. His 8,804 total career rushing yards were the third-best in high school history.

Now Emmitt had a decision to make. Where would he attend college?

At first, he narrowed his choices to six colleges: Nebraska, Clemson, Florida State, Alabama, Auburn, and the University of Florida. According to the rules of the National Collegiate Athletic Association, or NCAA, he was then allowed to visit each campus.

After the visits, Emmitt narrowed down his choices to Auburn, Nebraska, and Florida. He then decided it was too cold in Nebraska, leaving Auburn and Florida in the hunt.

Both schools pulled out all the stops in an effort to get Emmitt to accept a scholarship. Auburn invited him to attend the Citrus Bowl and had Emmitt introduced to the crowd. He even met star Auburn running back Bo Jackson. At the same time, Florida coach Galen Hall promised Emmitt that if he attended Florida, he would start right away.

The accolades started piling on. He was named the Gatorade High School Player of the Year, which earned him a trip to the Super Bowl. *Parade* magazine also named him Player of the Year. Emmitt was even selected to visit the White House and met President Reagan as a representative of high school sports in the "Just Say No" anti-drug campaign.

But at the same time, Emmitt started hearing from his detractors. People from some of the schools he had decided not to attend started talking down his accomplishments. They whispered that he was too small and too slow to make it big as a college running back.

Several high school recruiting services jumped on the bandwagon. One service wrote that Emmitt was "a lugger, not a runner" and that "sportswriters blew him all out of proportion." Another complained that Emmitt's speed in the 40-yard dash was only 4.55 seconds. A number of other backs ran 4.4s or 4.3s.

Fortunately for Emmitt, Coach Pat Dye of Auburn and Galen Hall of Florida had already decided that he was for real. They agreed with what Coach Thomas thought. When a reporter once questioned him about Emmitt's speed, he responded simply, "I didn't see him get caught from behind very often."

As impressed as Thomas was with Emmitt's running ability, it was his behavior and personality that really made a lasting impression. As Thomas recalled later, "He [Emmitt] never missed a practice, never was late for a meeting, and I never heard him say a swear word. What you have to understand about Emmitt is that he didn't have to go out searching about who he was. . . . Emmitt knew who he was because he had a mother and father at home. He was very secure. All he had to worry about was who he could be. He could maximize his talents."

Emmitt's parents allowed him to make his own decision. "Go wherever you want to," said his father. "Just make sure you study." After thinking long and hard, Emmitt made his decision on February 11, 1987. At a press conference held in the Escambia High gym, Emmitt announced he had accepted a scholarship from University of Florida in Gainesville, Florida. In the end, he wanted to stay in Florida so his parents would have every opportunity to see him play.

Besides, grinned the former Escambia High Gator at the press conference, the University of Florida nickname was the Gators.

"Once a Gator, always a Gator," joked Emmitt.

Chapter Three:

1987-89

College Days

Soon after Emmitt Smith arrived in Gainesville in the summer of 1987, he began to realize just exactly what being a Gator meant. When the team held a "media day" for the players to meet local newspaper sportswriters and broadcasters, one journalist asked him, "How does it feel to be a savior?"

The question made Emmitt uncomfortable, but the perception was correct. The University of Florida football team competed in the Southeastern Conference, or SEC. One of the best college conferences in the country, its members include such perennial powers as Alabama, Louisiana State University, Auburn, and Georgia. Before Emmitt arrived, Florida had won the conference championship only once, in 1984, and even then was forced to give up the crown after it was discovered the university had broken some rules.

Because of the infractions, the school played several seasons under NCAA sanctions that restricted recruiting and prevented the team from making postseason appearances. The sanctions expired in 1987. With Emmitt Smith on board, everyone expected a return to winning ways.

The Gators opened their season on the road against the Miami Hurricanes on September 5. The Hurricanes, coached by Jimmy Johnson (a man with whom Emmitt would later become quite familiar), had finished the 1986 season ranked number two in the country. They were favorites to win the national championship in 1987.

Despite having worked out with the first team in practice, Emmitt started the game on the bench. He was shocked.

He watched in disbelief as Hurricanes wide receiver Michael Irvin shredded the Florida defense. Emmitt wasn't put in the game until late in the fourth quarter. Florida lost, 31–4.

It was the first game in his career that he had not started. This was something new for Emmitt Smith.

He knew that he could charge into Coach Hall's office to complain, but he also knew that wasn't the right way to handle the situation. He kept quiet and promised himself to make the most of any opportunity. He knew that if Florida kept losing, that opportunity would eventually come.

The next week at practice, Coach Hall approached him. "I know you're wondering why I didn't start you," he said. "I thought the pressure might be too much. I didn't want you to make a mistake and lose your confidence."

Emmitt Smith just looked at the coach for a moment, then said quietly, "How will you know if I'm a good football player if you don't throw me out there into a pressure situation and see how I'll respond?"

"You're right," agreed Hall.

The next week, the Gators played Tulsa. Emmitt didn't start, but he entered the game midway through the first half.

It didn't take him long to get going. He took a pitchout from Florida quarterback Kerwin Bell and looked upfield.

It was just like high school. Although the players

were bigger and faster, Emmitt Smith could still anticipate what was going to happen a split second before anyone else. He started running, stutter-stepped as a defender ran past him, cut back, lowered his head to avoid another tackle, and broke into the clear. Sixty yards later, he crossed the goal line with the first touchdown of his collegiate career.

That did it. From that moment on, Emmitt Smith was Florida's starting tailback. He finished the game with 109 yards rushing and added a second touchdown.

A week later, the Gators played powerful Alabama on national television. Millions of viewers from around the country tuned in to watch the battle between the Gators' Kerwin Bell and Alabama quarterback Bobby Humphries, both of whom were leading candidates to win the Heisman Trophy, the award given out each year to the best player in college football.

They saw the best player in college football that day, but his name wasn't Bell or Humphries. His name was Smith.

Emmitt Smith carried the ball 39 times that day for 224 yards and two touchdowns as he helped the Gators control the ball and keep it away from Alabama's powerful offense. Florida won, 23–14.

His 224-yard total was the most in Florida history. Emmitt was on a roll.

He seemed to improve each week, although he failed to gain 200 yards again as Florida started winning big. In his seventh game of the season, he broke the 1,000-yard barrier. No freshman running back in the history of college football had ever reached 1,000 yards so quickly.

All of a sudden, he was even more famous. Florida was ranked in the Top Twenty, and people were talking about Emmitt Smith as a possible Heisman Trophy candidate.

But the Gators played a punishing schedule. On consecutive weeks they played SEC powerhouses Auburn and Georgia, then finished the season against cross-state rival Florida State.

The youthful Gators weren't quite prepared. They lost all three games. Emmitt managed to break 100 yards only in the season finale. Still, based primarily on the interest Emmitt Smith generated among football fans all over the country, the Gators were selected to play in the Aloha Bowl in Hawaii against

UCLA. Emmitt and his teammates hoped to finish on a high note.

It was not to be, as UCLA dumped Florida, 20–16, for the Gators' fourth consecutive loss. Emmitt managed to gain 128 yards but was no longer a legitimate candidate for the Heisman Trophy. He finished ninth in the balloting.

Still, Emmitt Smith looked forward to his sophomore season. He expected the Gators to improve, and he knew he would play better. So far, he had improved every year he had played football.

But he soon received a sign that his second season in Florida wouldn't go quite as smoothly as his first.

One night in the spring of his freshman year, Emmitt attended a fraternity party with several teammates. After a short time, he left the party to check out another party down the street. When he returned, he saw a crowd on the street outside. His teammates were arguing with some members of the fraternity.

He tried to break up the argument and was pulling one of his teammates toward his car when a drunken student stood in his way and insulted him, calling him a racist name. Emmitt pushed the young man, but one of his teammates threw a punch.

All of a sudden, everyone was fighting. Just as quickly, it appeared to be over.

Then Emmitt Smith and his teammates made a bad decision. Instead of allowing the fight to be forgotten, they went to their dorm and told some other football players what had just happened. With nearly a dozen reinforcements, they returned to the fraternity house looking for a fight.

They found one. Several students ended up being taken away by ambulance, and several players were arrested. When the story hit the newspapers, it wasn't reported as "Twelve Florida football players got into a fight last night," it was "*Emmitt Smith* and eleven of his teammates got into a fight last night."

Although Emmitt hadn't hit anyone, he was embarrassed. The media started referring to the players as "the dirty dozen" and acted as if Emmitt Smith were the head of a gang. He had to call his parents to explain everything. He also promised himself to be a little smarter.

The Gators got off to a quick start the following

fall, destroying Montana State, 69–0, and Indiana State, 58–0, in the first two games of the season. Emmitt hardly played in the second half of either game and still rushed for well over 100 yards in each.

But the Gators had changed their offense in the off-season. Inexplicably, they had decided to throw the ball more. When they began playing other teams in the conference, Emmitt Smith started getting the ball less and less. Often, he was used as a decoy for the passing game.

He was less than thrilled but couldn't argue with the results. At midseason, the Gators were undefeated and ranked fourteenth in the country.

Their sixth game was against Memphis State. Early in the game Emmitt got the ball behind the line of scrimmage. He saw a narrow hole and tried to bust through.

Just as he hit the line, the hole started to close. A tackler hit him head-on.

The two collided violently, but Emmitt Smith refused to fall down. He absorbed the blow, stood straight up, and tried to regain his momentum.

He wasn't moving forward or backward. In fact,

his legs weren't moving at all. For a split second, he was standing still.

Then another player blasted in from the side. His shoulder hit the back of Emmitt's knee.

If he had been moving his legs, the blow would have knocked him over harmlessly. But with all his weight planted on one leg, his knee took the force of the blow.

Pop! Emmitt heard a sickening sound come from his knee as he collapsed to the ground. He knew immediately that he was hurt. He had to be helped from the field.

Emmitt Smith had never been seriously injured before, and a thousand thoughts swarmed through his head. What if I can't play anymore? he wondered. Then he remembered his father's admonition when he was trying to decide where to go to school — "Just make sure you study."

Now he understood. Football could end in an instant. His purpose in college was to get an education. Even though he had been doing okay so far, Emmitt promised himself to pay a little more attention to his studies.

Fortunately, he had only stretched a ligament in

41

his knee. He would not have to undergo surgery. The team doctor said that in another four to six weeks, Emmitt Smith would be able to play again.

He healed quickly and returned to the lineup in four weeks. By then it was too late. Without him, the Gators lost twice. Then, when he finally did return, he had to wear a heavy brace and didn't run as well as he had before. The Gators lost to Georgia, then were slaughtered by Florida State, 52–17. For the second year in a row, the Gators had finished the regular season with a big losing streak.

The defeats demoralized the entire team. Before the season ended, some of the players were in open rebellion against the coaching staff. They were particularly displeased with the team's offensive coordinator, whom they blamed for their poor offensive performance.

Still, with a 6–5 record, the Gators received an invitation to play Illinois in the All-American Bowl in Birmingham, Alabama. They somehow managed to come together and defeat the Illini, 14–10. Emmitt was especially pleased, as he ran for 159 yards and scored both touchdowns, including a 55-yard scamper. His knee had completely healed, and he was running as well as he ever had.

Emmitt Smith looked forward to the upcoming season. He hoped that after two frustrating seasons, the Gators had turned the corner. Maybe next year, he thought to himself, maybe next year we'll be better.

Chapter Four:
1989

Decision Time

In the off-season, the team changed its offense again, so the players had to learn yet another entirely new system. At first, Emmitt Smith was concerned. He was afraid he wouldn't get to carry the ball very much.

But the new offensive coordinator, Whitey Jordan, loved running the football. He had once coached running back Eric Dickerson, who had gone on to become a star in the NFL. Jordan appreciated Emmitt Smith and made sure the Gators kept putting the ball into his hands.

He took full advantage of the opportunity. Although the Gators narrowly lost to Mississippi in their season opener, Emmitt gained 117 yards and scored twice. Then he gained more than 100 yards in the next two games, both victories, including 182 yards against Memphis State.

After the Memphis State game, Emmitt Smith met with his parents. He expected them to be happy with his performance. Instead, his father greeted him with a stern look.

After scoring one of his touchdowns, Emmitt had "celebrated" in the end zone by doing a little dance. He had never done so before, but his teammates had encouraged him to do something to quiet Memphis State's raucous fans. Emmitt Smith Jr., however, had not enjoyed the spectacle.

"You don't need to be doing that type of thing," he admonished his son. "You've been in the end zone hundreds of times. Why start acting like you've never seen one before?"

Emmitt decided that his father was right. He abandoned the dance and eventually decided to celebrate his touchdowns in a unique and understated way. If you watch Emmitt Smith score a touchdown today, all he does is remove his helmet. It is as if he is saying, "Don't you recognize me? Here I am again."

The Gators played LSU the following week. It was a tough and punishing game. Emmitt banged out 117 yards on the ground, and the Gators won on a last-second field goal, 16–13. Finally, he thought, we're on our way.

One day later, the team was shocked to learn that Coach Galen Hall had resigned. The university's basketball program was already under investigation by the NCAA for recruiting violations, and that investigation had just been expanded to include the football program. Hall had apparently decided to resign rather than fight. He was replaced by assistant Gary Darnell.

The charges rocked the football program, but the Gators kept winning. A few weeks later, though, several players, including both the starting and second-string quarterbacks, were suspended from the team.

It was up to Emmitt Smith to keep the team going. He responded brilliantly.

After rushing for 202 yards to help defeat Vanderbilt (the most yards he had gained in a game since facing Alabama in his freshman season), he set a new career record against New Mexico State.

Forced to start a freshman at quarterback, the Gators had to run on almost every play. Time after time, the ball was put in Emmitt's hands.

He ran every way he knew how — blasting over

defenders, running around them, and faking them out of their shoes. When the game ended, Florida had a hard-earned 27–21 victory, and Emmitt Smith had a new Florida rushing record — 316 yards!

But after defeating Kentucky one week later (with Emmitt adding another 126 yards to his season total), the Gators ran out of steam. For the third year in a row, they lost to Auburn, Georgia, and Florida State, finishing the regular season a disappointing 7–4.

The team still received a bowl bid, this time to the Freedom Bowl, in Anaheim, California, to face the University of Washington. But the game wasn't even close. Washington held Emmitt to less than 100 yards rushing and blew out the Gators, 34–7.

Emmitt Smith still finished the year with 1,599 rushing yards and 14 touchdowns. Entering his senior year, he would be the odds-on favorite to win the Heisman Trophy.

But Emmitt Smith had to make a decision. In April 1990, for the first time ever, college juniors would be eligible for the NFL draft. If he wanted to, he could go pro.

Just after the Freedom Bowl, the University of

Florida decided to clean up the football program. Afraid of being sanctioned by the NCAA again, the university fired the entire football coaching staff and hired Steve Spurrier to be the Gators' new head coach.

As the Florida quarterback in 1966, Spurrier had won the Heisman Trophy. He had since earned a reputation as a fine coach who was particularly adept at developing a potent passing offense.

That troubled Emmitt. If Florida decided to build for the future and go with a passing game, he was afraid he'd be lost in the shuffle.

Still, he wasn't certain he was ready to leave school. He enjoyed college life and knew his parents wanted him to graduate. Emmitt Smith decided to meet with Spurrier and discuss the future.

The new coach neither asked him to leave nor tried to convince him to stay. Coach Spurrier appeared impatient and just wanted to know whether Emmitt had made up his mind or not. He made no attempt to convince Emmitt Smith to stay in school for his senior year.

The meeting left Emmitt a little confused. He

drove home almost three hundred miles to Pensacola and mulled over his options. Then he sat down with his parents and explained the situation.

He was surprised to learn that they understood his frustration. They told him that if he decided the time was right to turn professional, it was okay with them.

Then Emmitt Smith made a promise.

"I will get my college degree," he told them. "I promise that after I turn pro, I won't build a house until I get my college diploma."

Emmitt's mother just nodded. She didn't doubt her son, but she probably didn't realize the number of athletes who make similar promises, only to conveniently forget them once they become wealthy.

Then he drove back to Gainesville. On January 31, 1990, Emmitt Smith announced that he would enter the NFL draft and leave school after the spring semester. He was happy with his decision, but it also filled him with anxiety.

Because of the new rule allowing underclassmen to declare for the draft, there was more talent available to be drafted than ever before. In any other year,

Emmitt Smith would have been a certain first-round pick. But in 1990, it wasn't clear precisely when he would be drafted or by whom.

Just as some observers had questioned his ability when he left high school, some now questioned whether he would make it in the NFL. At only five foot nine, he was smaller than most NFL running backs. Some observers believed he would wear down after being knocked around by the huge linemen in the NFL.

Others still questioned his speed. Many players faster than Emmitt Smith had tried to make it professionally and had failed. Many thought it was risky to use a first-round draft pick on him.

But he had one factor in his favor. Despite the overall depth of the draft, it was abnormally weak at running back. Emmitt Smith and Blair Thomas of Penn State were clearly the two best runners available.

On the day of the draft, Emmitt and his family gathered at a friend's beach house to watch the draft on television.

Illinois quarterback Jeff George was selected first

by the Indianapolis Colts. Then Blair Thomas was picked by the New York Jets. All right, thought Emmitt, the next team that needs a running back will surely pick me.

Team after team made their picks. Most selected defensive players or offensive linemen. The first round was more than half over and he still hadn't been picked. He was so nervous that he had to leave the room and go outside.

Then Emmitt heard his mother calling him. Someone wanted to speak with him on the telephone.

It was the player personnel director of the Dallas Cowboys, Bob Ackles. "How would you like to be a Cowboy?" he asked.

Emmitt Smith's eyes turned huge, and a big grin broke out on his face. "I'd love it," he said. He couldn't believe that his favorite team was interested in drafting him. Ackles told him to stay by the phone and hung up.

Sixteen players had been selected so far. The Cowboys had the twenty-first pick in the draft. They had planned on picking a defensive player, but when they realized that Emmitt Smith was still available, they traded up for the seventeenth pick to make sure they could get him.

Then the phone rang again. This time it was Dallas coach Jimmy Johnson.

"Emmitt," he said, "how'd you like to wear a star on your helmet?"

"I'd love it," answered Emmitt.

Johnson told Emmitt that he was about to be drafted. Emmitt Smith and his family then watched on television as the Cowboys made their announcement.

The Gator was now a Cowboy.

Chapter Five:
1990

Rookie Cowboy

Emmitt Smith flew to Dallas immediately. Later that evening, he was introduced to the press and had a chance to meet coach Jimmy Johnson and Cowboys owner Jerry Jones.

It was Johnson who had decided to trade up to get Emmitt. While many teams worried about his speed, Coach Johnson did not. Before joining the Cowboys, he had served as head coach at the University of Miami. Miami and Florida played a similar schedule, so as he watched films of his opponents, Johnson had seen plenty of Emmitt Smith. As he later told a reporter, "There were all these people saying, 'He's too slow,' or 'He's too small.' Every time I saw a film of him, he was running for a touchdown."

Owner Jerry Jones concurred. On draft day, he told a radio commentator that even though Emmitt

Smith had lasted until the seventeenth pick, as far as the Cowboys were concerned, "he was the fourth-best player in the draft."

Although being drafted by the Cowboys fulfilled one of Emmitt Smith's childhood dreams, it was far from an ideal situation. Under Coach Johnson, the Cowboys were rebuilding. The previous season, they had won only once in sixteen games. The local press was critical of almost everything the Cowboys did. The selection of Emmitt Smith was no exception.

Many members of the local media still thought he was too slow, and they believed the Cowboys should have selected a defensive player. Others felt that all Emmitt Smith could do was run and that the Cowboys should have picked a running back who had also proved himself as a receiver. Others focused on the fight at the frat party and wondered whether he would be able to stay out of trouble.

Then he and the Cowboys couldn't reach an agreement on a contract. The criticism of Emmitt Smith escalated.

His agent used Jones's statement about Emmitt Smith's being the fourth-best player in the draft to argue that he should be paid as such. The Cowboys disagreed.

As summer started to turn to fall, training camp began and Emmitt Smith was nowhere to be seen. Although he had moved into a small apartment in Dallas, he finally returned to Gainesville and enrolled in school for his senior year, just as he had promised his mother. He wanted the Cowboys to know that if he didn't get the contract he felt he deserved, he'd go back to school.

The two sides finally reached an agreement on September 4, only five days before the Cowboys opened the regular season. Emmitt Smith signed a three-year contract worth a total of 3 million dollars.

He was pleased with the money, but he was more pleased that the negotiations were over. He wanted to play football.

When he finally joined the team, Emmitt was way behind. He did his best to catch up. In practice that week, he worked hard, asked questions, and stayed quiet. He didn't want any of the veteran players to think he had a bad attitude.

Yet, despite his late start, playing for the Cowboys did present some opportunities. Coach Johnson believed in Emmitt Smith. Since the Cowboys were a young team, he was certain to receive a chance to succeed. Moreover, the team already had a nucleus of good, young players — quarterback Troy Aikman, receiver Michael Irvin, guard Nate Newton, and linebacker Ken Norton. They only needed to gain experience and self-confidence.

Sitting in his apartment the night before the season opener, Emmitt recalled the words of Coach Thomas: "It's a dream until you write it down. Then it's a goal." Before almost every game in high school and college, Emmitt Smith had paused for a moment to write down what he hoped to accomplish.

He did so again. On a piece of paper, he carefully wrote down, "Rookie of the Year," "Team's Leading Rusher," and "One Thousand Yards." As he finished, a teammate, rookie safety James Washington, dropped by for a visit.

Washington saw the scrap of paper on the counter. "What's this?" He giggled as he read out the list.

Emmitt didn't laugh. He took the list from Washington's hands and said solemnly, "This is what I want to accomplish this season."

But the next day, his goals remained dreams. In

the first game of the season, against San Diego, he sat on the bench for much of the game. The Dallas coaching staff didn't think he was prepared to play much.

He finally got into the game late in the fourth quarter. In the huddle, Troy Aikman called out the play, a run.

Aikman barked out the signals, took the snap, then spun around and pushed the ball into Emmitt's stomach. Emmitt Smith looked at the line and tried to find a hole.

There wasn't one. With the defense closing in, he simply put his head down and pushed forward as far as he could. The San Diego defense swarmed over him, and he disappeared under a pile of jerseys. He gained less than a yard.

One more carry yielded a similar result before the game ended. Dallas won, 17–14. Yet his brief appearance taught Emmitt Smith that pro football was much different from college ball. He couldn't believe how much faster and bigger the players were.

A week later, Emmitt Smith was named to the starting lineup. With 3 million dollars invested in him, the Cowboys wanted to get their money's worth.

Emmitt Smith made little difference in the game as the Cowboys lost to the New York Giants, 28–7. He carried the ball only six times for 11 yards and caught two short passes. The game became memorable only because of an altercation with star Giant linebacker Lawrence Taylor.

On one of his six carries, Smith ran around the end and was tackled by Taylor. As he made contact, the veteran decided to give the rookie an unforgettable welcome to the NFL. He swung out his huge fist and caught Emmitt's chin just beneath the faceguard.

He saw stars but stayed in the game. If he allowed Taylor to know that he was hurt, he would lose the respect of the opposition. If that happened, he would get hit with cheap shots at every opportunity.

The Cowboys were struggling. They were falling behind early, which forced them to go to their passing game. There simply wasn't time to work Emmitt Smith into the offense.

Not until the fifth game of the season did he get a real chance to shine. Against the 3–1 Tampa Bay Buccaneers, the Cowboy coaches told him that they planned to run the ball.

The Dallas defense kept the game close, and the

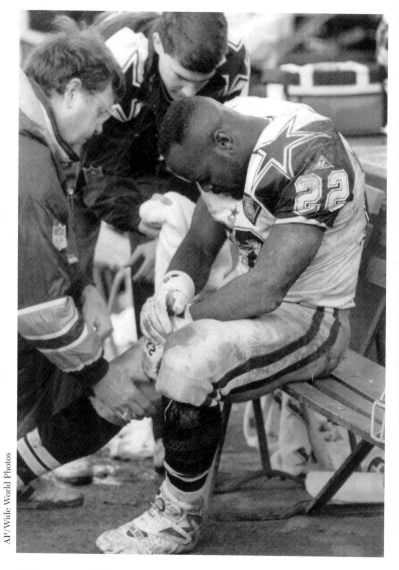

A leg injury sidelines Emmitt Smith in January 1995.

Emmitt Smith cradles his third rushing trophy.

On his way to a touchdown, Emmitt Smith leaves a flock of Philadelphia Eagles behind.

Emmitt Smith goes up and over for another Dallas gain.

On his way to breaking the NFL single-season touchdown record, Emmitt Smith wrestles free of a tackle.

With a mighty charge, Emmitt Smith crosses the goal line to give Dallas six more points.

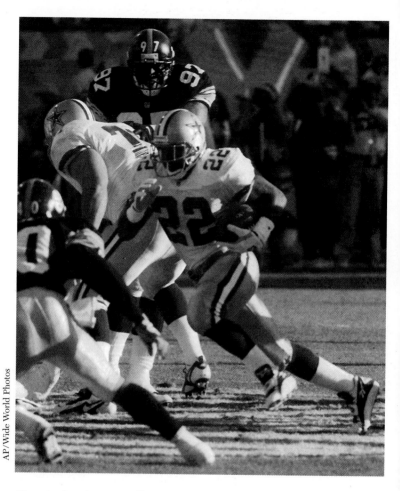

Emmitt Smith starts off Super Bowl XXX with a 23-yard run against the Pittsburgh Steelers.

With a smile a mile wide, Emmitt Smith reminds the crowd that the Cowboys have three Super Bowl victories.

Emmitt Smith's Year-by-Year Statistics

Year/Team	Attempts	Yards	Average	Touchdowns
1987—88 Florida	229	1,341	5.9	13
1988—89 Florida	189	988	5.3	9
1989—90 Florida	284	1,599	5.6	14
COLLEGE TOTALS	700	3,928	5.6	36
1990—91 Cowboys	241	937	3.9	11
1991—92 Cowboys	365	1,563	4.3	12
1992—93 Cowboys	373	1,713	4.6	18
1993—94 Cowboys	283	1,486	5.3	9
1994—95 Cowboys	368	1,484	4.0	21
1995—96 Cowboys	377	1,773	4.7	25
1996—97 Cowboys	327	1,204	3.7	12
PRO TOTALS 7 years	2,334	10,160	4.4	108

Emmitt Smith's Career Highlights

1986: Named High School Player of the Year by *USA Today* and *Parade* magazine

1987: Named All-SEC and All-American at Florida

1988: Named All-SEC and All-American at Florida

1989: Named All-SEC and All-American at Florida

1990–91: NFL Rookie of the Year
Selected to play in the Pro Bowl

1991–92: NFL rushing champion
Selected to play in the Pro Bowl

1992–93: NFL rushing champion
Selected to play in the Pro Bowl
Member of Super Bowl XXVII championship team

1993–94: NFL rushing champion
Named NFL Most Valuable Player
Member of Super Bowl XXVIII
  championship team
Named Super Bowl XXVIII MVP

1995–96: NFL rushing champion
Member of Super Bowl XXX championship team

Holds NFL records for:
- Most rushing touchdowns in single season (25)
- Most rushing touchdowns in the Super Bowl, career (5)

coaching staff kept their promise. Emmitt Smith rushed for 121 yards, his first game as a pro for more than 100 yards. The Cowboys practiced ball control and won, 14–10.

Emmitt hoped his performance would guarantee him a featured role in the Cowboys' offense, but it didn't happen. It was the same old story as the Cowboys dropped four of their next five games. They fell behind early, and Emmitt Smith hardly touched the ball.

He was growing impatient. Some members of the press were still questioning his talent, and the Cowboys' passing attack was struggling. Emmitt knew that the only way he could prove himself and help Aikman succeed was for the Cowboys to let him run the ball enough to take pressure off the passing game. It was time, he decided, to start complaining.

Before the next game, he approached running back coach Joe Brodsky and told him straight-out, "We need to gain a hundred yards on the ground." In the Cowboys' next game, against the Los Angeles Rams, Emmitt Smith got his chance.

He carried the ball 21 times. Although he gained only 54 yards, he also caught four passes for 117 yards. The performance forced the Rams to pay attention to him and allowed Troy Aikman to have his best game as a pro. Dallas won, 24–21.

For the rest of the season, Emmitt Smith was a big part of the Cowboys' offense. Against Washington one week later, he gained a season-high 132 yards.

The game was broadcast nationally. One play had everyone talking about Emmitt Smith the next day.

Late in the fourth quarter, with the Cowboys clinging to a slim three-point lead and the ball on the Washington 48-yard line, Emmitt Smith took a handoff from Troy Aikman. The play was supposed to run off right guard.

Emmitt saw the hole open and charged toward it, but he also saw the Redskins' secondary overreact to the play. As soon as he burst through the hole, he cut back sharply to his left. The Washington defense scrambled to change direction.

He headed down the left sideline, leaving most of the defenders behind. Only one man was in position to catch him. Veteran Washington cornerback Darrell Green hadn't overreacted. He had the angle and was charging fast.

Emmitt Smith had two choices. He could try to

put a move on Green and avoid the tackle. But then the other pursuers might catch up and tackle him from behind. Or he could try to stiff-arm Green. If it worked, he might score. If it didn't, he'd likely be stopped in his tracks.

He decided on the stiff-arm. As Green approached, Smith tucked the ball firmly under his left arm and put his right arm out for balance. When Green put his head down and charged to make the tackle, Emmitt placed his right hand on the cornerback's helmet and pushed off.

It worked! The stiff-arm pushed Green to the ground, and Emmitt Smith pivoted past him without breaking stride. He rolled into the end zone to give the Cowboys an insurance touchdown. They won, 27–17.

The play impressed pro football fans all over the country. The way he cleverly picked his way through the line reminded some of Chicago Bears great Walter Payton, while others compared his acceleration to Emmitt's old hero, Tony Dorsett. But the stiff-arm had reminded everyone of Earl Campbell, a star running back for the Houston Oilers in the late 1970s and early 1980s. No running back since Campbell had used the crowd-pleasing stiff-arm as effectively as Emmitt Smith.

Keyed by their rookie running back, the Cowboys surged in the second half of the season, winning four games in a row to take their record to 7–7. With two games remaining, they had an outside chance to make the playoffs.

Then disaster struck. Troy Aikman separated his shoulder. Now the Cowboys had no passing game at all. Opposing defenses simply focused on Emmitt Smith. They shut him down, and the Cowboys lost twice to finish the season with a record of 7–9. There would be no playoff games for Dallas in 1990.

Still, Emmitt Smith had accomplished many of his goals. Although he finished just shy of 1,000 yards, with 937, he had led the team in rushing and was named Rookie of the Year by several different organizations. He was even selected to play in the Pro Bowl, the only Dallas player to make the team.

He had survived his first season in the NFL. But there were more goals waiting for him up ahead.

Chapter Six:
1991–92

Turning the Corner

Before the 1991 season, the Cowboys made several changes. In 1990, the offense had ranked last among the twenty-eight teams of the NFL. So they demoted offensive coordinator David Shula and replaced him with Norv Turner. When Emmitt Smith met Turner for the first time, he went right up to the coach with a big smile on his face and asked, "Are you gonna give me the ball this year, or what?"

Turner just laughed and told Emmitt he had nothing to worry about. That's all he needed to hear. He just wanted a chance. If he got one, he was convinced he would come through.

Dallas coach Jimmy Johnson had precisely the same attitude entering the upcoming season. He told his team, "Not only will we make the playoffs, but we will have success in the playoffs." As far as

Johnson was concerned, being competitive wasn't good enough anymore. He expected the Cowboys to win.

Emmitt Smith had his goals, too. When he wrote down before the season what he hoped to accomplish, he added "NFL Rushing Title" to the list.

In the first game of the season, Emmitt Smith and the rest of the Cowboys proved they were up to the task. Facing the always difficult Cleveland Browns in Cleveland, the Cowboys ground out a tough 26–14 win.

Emmitt Smith was magnificent. As Turner had promised, the Cowboys kept putting the ball in his hands. He carried the ball 32 times and caught six passes. Although he gained only 112 yards on the ground, his performance permitted the Cowboys to control the ball for a long time, keeping Cleveland off the field and allowing the Cowboys to protect their lead.

He followed that performance one week later by exploding for a 75-yard touchdown run against the Washington Redskins. But during the second half, he became sick to his stomach and had to leave the game. The Cowboys lost a heartbreaker, 33–31.

After losing their second game in a row the next week, the Cowboys suddenly caught fire, winning five of six. Emmitt Smith keyed the surge with his spectacular running, including a 182-yard game against Phoenix on September 22.

After nine games, the Cowboys were 6–3, in the middle of the playoff hunt. Emmitt Smith was averaging more than 100 yards per game and was among the NFL leaders in rushing yardage.

In Week Ten, the Cowboys faced the Houston Oilers, their intrastate rivals. At 7–2, the Oilers were also looking forward to the playoffs.

Through four quarters, the two teams played each other even. Tied at 23, the game went into overtime.

The Cowboys got the ball and started driving downfield. They were well within field goal range when they handed the ball to Emmitt Smith one last time.

Since Dallas was already within field goal range, his priorities should have been to protect the ball first, then worry about gaining yardage. But he just couldn't help himself. He wanted to score a game-winning touchdown. When the Oilers tackled him, instead of going down, he struggled forward and lost his grip on the ball. Fumble!

Houston recovered. Quarterback Warren Moon marched them down the field, and the Oilers kicked a field goal to win, 26–23.

Emmitt felt terrible. He knew his miscue had cost his team the game.

He tried to make up for that mistake the following week against the New York Giants, but the harder he tried, the worse he played. He made two critical fumbles, and the Giants won, 22–9. Suddenly, the Cowboys were only 6–5. They were in danger of not making the playoffs.

Their schedule wasn't getting any easier, either. Their next opponent, the Washington Redskins, were 11–0.

The Cowboys fell behind 7–0 in the first quarter. On third down at the 34-yard line, Dallas coach Jimmy Johnson knew he had to gamble. He crossed up the Redskins and called a draw play for Emmitt Smith.

A draw play is a run designed to start out looking like a pass. When the ball is snapped, the running back just stays in place and pretends to pass-block.

The quarterback drops back as if to pass, the wide receivers race downfield, and the offensive line steps back to create a protective pocket around the quarterback.

Then the quarterback hands off the ball. By this time, the defense thinks the play is a pass. If the running back can make it through the line of scrimmage, the middle of the field is usually wide-open.

That's just what happened. Emmitt burst through the line, then charged down the middle of the field for a game-tying touchdown.

The rest of the game was a seesaw battle. Even when Troy Aikman injured his knee in the second half, the Cowboys kept it a close game. They won, 24–21, to keep their playoff hopes alive.

With Aikman out of the lineup, the Cowboys' offense depended on Emmitt Smith. Over the final five games of the season, including the Washington game, he averaged more than 30 carries per game. The Cowboys won all five and vaulted into the playoffs.

In their first playoff appearance since 1985, the Cowboys defeated the Chicago Bears, 17–13, in the first round. Emmitt Smith became the first running back, ever, to rush for more than 100 yards against the Bears in a playoff game. Scheduled to face the Detroit Lions in round two, the Cowboys may have started looking ahead to a potential rematch against the Redskins for the NFC championship.

It was not to be. The Lions took control early and beat Dallas in every way possible, 38–6. The Cowboys' season was over.

Yet, despite the loss, they still accomplished much of what they had set out to do. As Johnson had promised, the Cowboys made the playoffs and had some success. And Emmitt Smith reached his personal goal. He won the NFL rushing title with 1,563 yards.

But a new season meant new goals. Johnson challenged his team to win the Super Bowl. So Emmitt added a Super Bowl win to his own list. He and the Cowboys couldn't wait for the 1992 season to begin.

In the off-season, the team traded for San Francisco defensive lineman Charles Haley and defensive back Thomas Everett, solidifying the defense. Dallas began the 1992 season as bona fide Super Bowl contenders.

The Cowboys faced their first test in the season opener against the defending Super Bowl champs, the Washington Redskins. Even though it was only the first game of the season, Dallas knew the Redskins game was important. Both teams were in the same division. It would be almost impossible for the Cowboys to reach the Super Bowl without beating Washington.

Dallas passed the test with flying colors. The Cowboys shredded the Redskins' defense for nearly 400 total yards. Emmitt Smith gained 140 yards all by himself. Dallas won, 23–10, and set its sights on the Super Bowl.

From the first week, the Cowboys were clearly one of the best teams in pro football. They roared through the remainder of the regular season and entered the final week with a stellar 12–3 record.

Emmitt Smith was a big reason why the Cowboys were so good. Every time they needed him to pick up a first down or keep a drive going, he did. He even added pass-catching to his offensive repertoire, as he finished third on the team in receiving, with 59 catches. Entering the final game against Chicago, all of his preseason goals were still within reach.

Earlier that day, Pittsburgh running back Barry Foster had ended his season with a total of 1,690 yards rushing. Emmitt Smith began the day with 1,582 yards, knowing he needed 108 yards to catch Foster and capture his second consecutive NFL rushing title.

He knew it wasn't going to be easy. Although the Bears had failed to make the playoffs, their defense, led by linebacker Mike Singletary and defensive end Richard Dent, was tough and experienced. They had nothing to lose and wanted to shut down Emmitt Smith.

The Bears' defense keyed on Smith, and the Cowboys played conservatively. They just kept giving the ball to him and hoped he would pass Foster without getting hurt.

Early in the third quarter, the Cowboys led by two touchdowns and had the ball on the Chicago 31-yard line. Emmitt Smith had already rushed for 100 yards. He needed only eight more to tie Foster.

On the next play, the Cowboys gave the ball to Emmitt Smith for the 373rd time that season. And for the 373rd time, he was a split second ahead of everyone else on the field.

He burst through the hole in the middle of the line, then cut back against the grain, eluding the Bears' linebackers. Then he headed upfield, zigging by one defensive back and zagging past another before taking aim at the end zone.

Crossing the goal line, he knew that the rushing title was his and that his day was over. Without breaking stride, he just kept running, right through the end zone and into the tunnel under the stands that leads to the dressing room, the ball tucked securely under his arm, and more than 60,000 Dallas fans roaring and cheering.

The Cowboys won, 27–14, to finish the regular season at 13–3. Emmitt Smith had accomplished one goal. There was one more he still wanted to reach.

Chapter Seven:
1992

Super Bowl–Bound

With the second-best regular-season record in the conference, the Cowboys had a bye in the first round of the playoffs. Coach Johnson gave the team a few days off, so Emmitt Smith went home to Pensacola and watched on television as the Philadelphia Eagles defeated New Orleans, 36–20, to earn the right to play the Cowboys.

The Philadelphia victory pleased the Cowboys. For years, Dallas has considered the Eagles and New York Giants its archrivals. With all three teams competing in the NFC's tough Eastern Division, their games have a special atmosphere.

In the week before the game, some Philadelphia players predicted victory. After all, they reasoned, the Eagles had been one of only three teams to defeat the Cowboys all year. In fact, the Eagles had slaughtered the Cowboys, 31–7, in the fourth game of the season.

But the Cowboys planned to be prepared. It would be the first playoff game at Texas Stadium in a decade. The players didn't want to let their fans down.

They didn't. The Cowboys dominated from the opening snap and won going away, 34–10. Emmitt Smith rushed for 114 yards, including 69 yards in the third quarter, when he scored his first postseason touchdown on a nifty 23-yard draw play. The win sent the Cowboys into the NFC Championship Game against San Francisco.

The 49ers' 14–2 regular-season record was the best in pro football that year. Led by quarterback Steve Young, wide receiver Jerry Rice, and running back Rickey Watters, the 49ers had the most powerful offense in the game. To win, the Cowboys knew they would have to either shut down the San Francisco offense or somehow find a way to outscore them.

The first half was close. Emmitt scored on a short touchdown plunge to put the Cowboys up, 10–7, but the 49ers kicked a field goal just before halftime to tie the score.

The Cowboys were convinced they could pass on the 49ers' defense. But throughout the first half, they had used Emmitt Smith to establish the run. Now they decided it was time to go to the air.

After the kickoff, they took over on their own 22-yard line. A series of play-action passes moved the ball down the field.

On a play-action pass, the quarterback fakes a handoff to a running back, trying to make the defense think the play is a run. Then he fades back and looks for a receiver. If the fake succeeds, there is usually a receiver open because the defensive backfield had moved up to tackle the player they thought was running the ball.

Emmitt's role in a play-action pass is simple. He pretends to take the handoff, then runs into the line, where he either helps pass-block or moves into the flat and becomes a "safety valve." If all other receivers are covered, the running back often is open.

Because the Cowboys had established the run in the first half, the 49ers had to pay attention to Emmitt Smith. Time after time, they fell for the fake, then scrambled to recover as Aikman faded back and found open receivers downfield. Fullback Darryl

"Moose" Johnston scored from the 3-yard line to put Dallas up, 17–10.

San Francisco came back and kicked a field goal to make the score 17–13. The Cowboys took the ensuing kickoff and returned it to their own 21.

Then the 49ers changed their defensive strategy, deciding to blitz and send the linebackers charging through the line. If the play was a run, they'd be in position to stop it. If it was a pass, they hoped to sack Aikman before he could throw the ball.

But the Cowboys were ready. They kept passing, and Aikman managed to get rid of the ball before the 49ers could get to him. They quickly moved into 49er territory.

At the San Francisco 16-yard line, Emmitt Smith drifted out to the right side as Troy Aikman dropped back. The quarterback saw that Smith was open and lofted the ball in his direction.

Emmitt gathered in the pass and ran into the end zone without being touched. Now the Cowboys' lead grew to 24–13.

Although San Francisco rallied to pull within four points at 24–20, the Cowboys hung on to win, 30–20. They were going to the Super Bowl!

In the American Football Conference, the Buffalo Bills won the championship and earned their third consecutive trip to the Super Bowl. After losing in the Super Bowl the past two years, they were determined not to lose again.

The two teams gathered in Pasadena, California, the site of Super Bowl XXVII, a week before the game. Super Bowl week is usually a swirl of publicity and hype. That year was no different.

In an interview a few days before the game, Emmitt Smith revealed a new goal. He didn't just want to win the game, he said, "I want to be the Super Bowl MVP." As game time approached, he was determined not to let his words come back to haunt him.

Buffalo stormed out in the first quarter. The Bills shut down the Cowboys on their opening possession, then blocked a punt and scored a quick touchdown to take an early 7–0 lead. The Cowboys had to regroup.

No one panicked. Although the Bills kicked off and shut down Dallas for a second time, the Cowboys' defense came through. On the Bills' next possession, Dallas intercepted Buffalo quarterback Jim Kelly and gave the offense another chance.

Dallas stuck with its game plan. This time the Cowboys moved smartly downfield, mixing runs by Emmitt Smith with some short passes. Troy Aikman hit tight end Jay Novacek with a 23-yard touchdown pass, and the Cowboys tied the score, 7–7.

After the kickoff, Buffalo made another mistake, fumbling deep in its own territory. Cowboy tackle Jimmie Jones picked up the ball and rumbled two yards into the end zone to put the Cowboys ahead, 14–7.

The rout was on. The Bills couldn't seem to hang on to the football, and the Cowboys took advantage of every mistake. Troy Aikman picked apart the Buffalo secondary and kept finding receivers in the end zone. At halftime, the Cowboys led 28–10.

The Cowboys had hardly needed him, but Emmitt Smith chipped in with his usual all-star performance. In the fourth quarter, with Dallas leading 38–17, he took the ball on a draw play at the 10-yard line and put the game out of reach as he broke several tackles and charged into the end zone.

As he crossed the goal line, he felt a huge feeling of satisfaction. He had proved his critics wrong at every step of his career and achieved most of his goals.

Although Troy Aikman, who had thrown four touchdown passes for the day, was named Super Bowl MVP, Emmitt didn't mind. He was happy just to win the game. He knew that was the most important goal of all.

In the final moments of the game, with Dallas leading 52–17, two of the Cowboys' huge linemen, Nate Newton and Charles Haley, sneaked up behind coach Jimmy Johnson with a huge bucket of Gatorade. They dumped it on his head in celebration.

The Cowboy players started to laugh and celebrate, then looked at Johnson in disbelief. His carefully combed hair, the object of much locker room humor, hadn't even moved!

That was too much for Emmitt Smith to take. He rushed over to Johnson, placed both hands on his head, and raked his fingers through the coach's hair. Then both men just looked at each other and laughed before embracing. It felt good to be on the winning team.

Chapter Eight:
1993

Holdout

Much had changed since Emmitt Smith had first joined the Cowboys. When he turned pro in 1990, he did so surrounded by questions concerning his ability. In three short years, he had answered his critics.

With more than 4,000 rushing yards in only three seasons, he was on a pace to become one of the greatest rushers in NFL history. He had made the Pro Bowl team three years in a row, had won the rushing titles the past two seasons, and had just become the first player, ever, to win both an NFL rushing title and the Super Bowl in the same season.

The three-year contract he signed as a rookie expired after the Super Bowl. Although he was widely considered to be the best running back in football, his old contract hadn't paid him like the best. Emmitt

Smith wanted his new contract to reflect his new status.

He told his agent that he wanted to be paid more money than any other non-quarterback in the league. He recognized that quarterbacks were always going to be the highest-paid players, but he wanted to make sure he didn't get shortchanged.

According to the rules, Emmitt Smith was a "restricted free agent," meaning that although he was free to negotiate with any team in the league, the Cowboys had the right to match any contract offer.

No other teams even bothered making him an offer. They were certain that Cowboy owner Jerry Jones would match it.

Although Emmitt was disappointed, he wasn't really upset. He preferred remaining with the Cowboys — but at the salary he thought he deserved.

Emmitt Smith and the Cowboys didn't have their first contract meeting until just before training camp. Emmitt asked for a four-year contract worth $17 million, just a little more than the one given to Green Bay defensive end Reggie White, the highest-paid non-quarterback in the league. The Cowboys countered with an offer of $9 million.

Both sides refused to budge. Dallas opened training camp without him. Then the preseason started. Emmitt Smith and the Cowboys remained far apart.

He returned to Pensacola to wait out the impasse. Since he had joined the Cowboys, Emmitt Smith had started his own business, Emmitt Incorporated, a company that employed his sister and parents and sold sports memorabilia. He helped manage the business, worked out at Escambia, and tried to stay in shape.

In the meantime, Dallas owner Jerry Jones tried to act as if the Cowboys didn't need Emmitt, telling the press, "Emmitt Smith is a luxury, not a necessity. The Cowboys can win the Super Bowl without Emmitt Smith."

That made Emmitt Smith angry. So far, he considered the contract impasse to be just business. He didn't appreciate being personally insulted. Jones's statement only made him more determined to get the contract he wanted.

Just before the season started, he offered to sign for less total money, but for fewer years. The Cowboys turned him down. They knew if they signed him to only a one- or two-year contract, when it expired,

Emmitt Smith would become a free agent. They wanted to keep him, but on their own terms.

Dallas opened the season on Monday night against the Redskins in Washington. Emmitt watched on television from Pensacola.

He could hardly believe it. In the tailback position stood Derrick Lassic, a rookie. Still, he hoped his teammates would defeat the Redskins.

Without him, they played one of their worst games in two years, losing 35–16. Lassic didn't play well at all.

Jerry Jones started to panic. He offered a four-year deal worth $12 million.

Emmitt said no. That Sunday, the Cowboys faced Buffalo in a rematch of the Super Bowl.

Jerry Jones's earlier statement came back to haunt him. With Emmitt Smith, the Cowboys had obliterated Buffalo in Super Bowl XXVII. Playing without him only eight months later, they lost, 13–10.

In the Dallas locker room after the game, several players got angry. Lassic had made a critical fumble that had helped cost Dallas the game. Defensive lineman Charles Haley slammed his helmet against the wall and raged, "We cannot win with a rookie running back!" With an 0–2 record, the Cowboys were in last place in the NFC's Eastern Division. Both the New York Giants and the Philadelphia Eagles had started the season 2–0. Dallas faced an uphill climb to make the playoffs.

Emmitt Smith and the Cowboys started talking again. After a few days of negotiations, Jerry Jones finally raised his offer to $13.6 million. Emmitt, afraid the season was slipping away, signed. Now he had a few new goals.

No NFL running back had ever won the rushing title after missing the first two games of the season. And no team had ever won the Super Bowl after losing its first two games.

Emmitt Smith wanted to make history.

Chapter Nine:

1993

The Super Season

Three days after he rejoined the team, Emmitt Smith and the Cowboys traveled to Phoenix to play the Cardinals. Derrick Lassic started the game, but just knowing that Emmitt was back made everyone play better. Lassic ran for 60 yards, and the Cowboys won, 17–10. Emmitt Smith got into the game late in the second half and added 48 yards on eight carries.

He was in the starting lineup a week later for the Cowboys' home game against Green Bay. All of a sudden, the Cowboys started playing like world champions again.

They blew out the Packers, 36–14. Although Emmitt gained only 71 yards, his presence forced Green Bay to respect the Cowboys' running game. That left Michael Irvin, Jay Novacek, and the other Dallas receivers wide-open. Troy Aikman took advantage and threw for more than 300 yards. The Cowboys were back!

A week later, in a win over Indianapolis, Emmitt Smith broke the 100-yard barrier for the first time all season. Ever so slowly, he was gaining on the other running backs in the race for the rushing title. At the same time, the Cowboys were gaining on the first-place New York Giants and second-place Philadelphia Eagles!

On October 31, the Cowboys traveled to Philadelphia to play the Eagles in a critical contest. After starting out strong, Philadelphia had stumbled to fall into a tie with Dallas at 4–2. With a win, the Cowboys could move into second place all by themselves.

The game began in a driving rainstorm. That didn't bother Emmitt Smith. He liked playing in the rain. In high school, some of his best games had been on days it rained.

He got off to a quick start and then accelerated. In the first half he raced for more than 100 yards as the Cowboys took a 10–0 lead.

But the Eagles came back in the second half. With just a few minutes remaining, Dallas led by only six points, 16–10.

Dallas had the ball on its own 38-yard line. On second and four, Coach Turner called for a draw play.

As Emmitt Smith lined up in the backfield, he looked out over the defense and had a familiar feeling. He could see what was going to happen.

He saw ten of the eleven Eagles bunched up at the line of scrimmage, anticipating a line plunge. Their lone defensive back followed a man in motion to the right side of the field. Emmitt knew that if he could make his way past the line, the field would be wide-open.

Troy Aikman took the snap from center and dropped back as if to pass. Emmitt Smith stood ready to receive the ball. The offensive line started pass-blocking and allowed the Philadelphia line to push wide on the left side. A big hole opened up.

Smith took the ball from Aikman and burst through the gap. Just as he had thought, as soon as he cleared the line of scrimmage, all he saw was open field.

He dashed downfield and broke to the sidelines, water splashing with each step, as the Eagles desperately tried to chase him down. But as his high school coach had noticed so long ago, Emmitt wasn't often caught from behind.

He raced 62 yards without being touched, to seal the win, 23–10. Dallas was now all alone in second place, and the Cowboys set their sights on the Giants. Emmitt Smith, with 237 total yards rushing for the day, his best performance as a Cowboy, took aim at the NFL rushing title.

Week after week, both the Giants and the Cowboys kept playing well. Both teams clinched a spot for postseason play. But in the next-to-last game of the regular season, New York lost to Phoenix as Dallas defeated Washington. That set up a final-week showdown between the two teams. At stake were the division championship and the home field advantage in the upcoming playoffs.

Meanwhile, Emmitt Smith had contributed a string of fabulous performances. He entered the game with a chance to capture the rushing title for the third year in a row. His goals were still within reach.

The two teams met on the frozen turf of Giants Stadium on January 2, 1994. Dallas broke loose early.

Emmitt keyed the attack. He ran roughshod over the New York defense, helping Dallas take a quick 10–0 lead.

Late in the second quarter, the Cowboys drove downfield again and had a chance to increase their lead. Troy Aikman handed the ball to Emmitt Smith for the nineteenth time that half on a play called the "Power Right." He burst through a huge hole carved out by the Cowboys' offensive line and dashed down the right sideline.

Only one player had a chance to catch him. New York safety Greg Jackson put his shoulder down and banged into Emmitt at the sideline as he fought for extra yardage.

Crunch! The two players hit in a bone-jarring collision. Fans throughout the stadium heard the two men making contact.

Emmitt Smith flew through the air and landed heavily on his right elbow. A sharp pain shot through his shoulder.

At first, his arm went numb. But a few moments later, he regained feeling. Yet he wasn't overly concerned. He often played with a little pain. He stayed in the game for the remainder of the half. Kicker

Eddie Murray booted a field goal as time ran out to give the Cowboys a 13–0 halftime lead.

During the break Emmitt realized that he was hurt more badly than he had thought. The slightest movement made his arm and shoulder throb. As his teammates returned to the field for the second half, he had an X-ray taken and waited anxiously for the results.

"You've got a grade-two shoulder separation," announced the team trainer.

"What's that mean?" asked Emmitt.

The trainer told him that he had separated his shoulder. While it was painful, there was little chance of further injury if he continued to play. The choice was his.

That's all he needed to hear. He directed the trainer to tape up his shoulder and returned to the field.

He hoped to gain a few more yards, then watch from the sidelines as his teammates went on to an easy win. But when Emmitt Smith jogged out the tunnel and onto the field, he heard the New York crowd roaring. The Cowboys were falling apart.

The Giants had just blocked a punt. A moment

later, they scored a touchdown, making the score 13–7. All of a sudden, the Cowboys were in a ball game.

Emmitt's priorities changed. From that moment on, he said later, "I never even considered the rushing title. I was out there to win."

Since he had done so well in the first half, the Cowboys decided to keep using him. As soon as they got the ball back, they put it in his hands.

Over and over again, he swept around the end or bulled his way through the line. Each time he was hit, he winced in pain.

Although he still picked up valuable yardage, the Cowboys couldn't score. The Giants kicked a field goal to make the score 13–10. Then, with only seconds remaining, they kicked a second field goal to tie the game.

Moments later, the gun went off signaling the end of regulation play. The game went into overtime.

That's just what Emmitt Smith needed. Not only was his shoulder hurt, but now his ribs and breastbone were bruised. It hurt to breathe, let alone run the football!

He told himself to ignore the pain. He knew that

if he left the game, the Giants would receive a huge emotional lift. He had to keep playing, he later remembered, "if only to pose the threat of a running game."

The Giants won the coin toss and received the kickoff to start overtime. Dallas stopped them, and New York was forced to punt. The Cowboys took over at their own 25-yard line.

In the huddle, all eyes were on him. His teeth were clenched and he moved stiffly.

"Emmitt, you okay?" asked one of the Cowboys.

"I'm fine!" he yelled.

Then, as they had so often in the past, the Cowboys turned to their all-Emmitt offense.

He carried the Cowboys downfield, running for tough yardage inside, sweeping the end, or catching Troy Aikman's passes. He tore the Giants' defense apart, pushing forward on each play despite the pain.

Finally, after carrying for ten more yards, he looked to the sidelines and saw that the Cowboys were within field goal range. "Get me out of here!" he barked to the sidelines.

The field goal unit charged onto the field as he

stiffly walked off. Placekicker Eddie Murray drilled a 41-yard field goal. The Cowboys won, 16–13. Emmitt Smith's day was done.

For the game, he gained an amazing 168 yards on 32 carries. He added another 61 yards on ten pass receptions. Of Dallas's 70 total offensive plays, Emmitt handled the ball 42 times, gaining 229 of the team's 339 yards. On the final, game-winning drive, he handled the ball on nine of eleven plays, gaining 41 of 52 yards.

"I don't know how he did it," wondered Cowboy guard Kevin Gogan after the game. "He sucked it up for his boys."

Afterward, an obviously pained Emmitt Smith met with reporters and explained his decision to keep playing. All he was thinking of, he said, was "win this game, plus winning the third rushing title."

He succeeded on both counts. Emmitt Smith finished with a season total of 1,486 rushing yards, more than enough to capture the NFL rushing title for the third consecutive year, becoming only the fourth player ever to do so.

When a reporter asked if he would be able to play in the first game of the playoff just two weeks away,

Emmitt Smith managed a weak smile. "There's no way," he said, "they'll keep me out of it."

He was right. Although some sportswriters and even some Dallas players thought Emmitt Smith was finished for the season, he proved them wrong. There was one more goal left for him to reach. The Super Bowl.

Although he was less than 100 percent healthy, Emmitt Smith at less than 100 percent is a better player than many others at full strength. Dallas beat Green Bay in the divisional playoffs, 28–17, as Emmitt Smith led players from both teams with 60 rushing yards. That set up another showdown with the dangerous 49ers, who had blown out the Giants, 44–3.

While nearly everyone was predicting that this was San Francisco's year, Emmitt reminded everyone that, so far anyway, the 1993 season had been his. He got the Cowboys going with a 5-yard touchdown run in the first quarter to give Dallas a 7–0 lead.

With Emmitt Smith setting the pace, the Cowboys scored touchdowns four of the first five times they got the ball. Emmitt racked up 88 yards rushing and gained 85 more receiving, again leading players on both teams in each category. Dallas won big, 38–21.

In the AFC, the Buffalo Bills made it to the Super Bowl for the fourth straight year. After three defeats, they were more determined than ever to win. But so was Emmitt Smith.

At first, it appeared as though the Bills would finally get their much-sought-after win. They moved the ball up and down the field with ease while shutting down the Dallas offense. At halftime, Buffalo led, 13–6.

Then the Cowboys decided to change strategy. Entering the game, they thought they could pass against the Buffalo secondary. But the Buffalo line, led by defensive end Bruce Smith, had pressured Troy Aikman into rushing his passes. The Dallas offense had sputtered.

"Troy needs time to throw the ball," said coach Jimmy Johnson at halftime. "We have to establish the run."

That brought a smile to Emmitt's face. He knew what that meant.

Early in the second half, the Cowboys got a break when Buffalo fumbled the ball at midfield. Cowboy defensive back James Washington scooped up the ball and scooted for a touchdown, tying the game.

Now the Cowboys had momentum. Their defense stopped Buffalo, and Dallas took over at its own 36.

Johnson made good on his promise. He directed Dallas offensive coordinator Norv Turner to call plays that put the ball in Emmitt Smith's hands.

He moved the Cowboys down the field as if he were a snowplow attacking drifts on a highway. On the eight-play drive, he ran the ball seven times. From the 15 he stormed around the end on a "Power Right" to score a touchdown and put the Cowboys ahead, 20–13.

Buffalo began to panic, and when a football team panics, it usually makes mistakes. Soon after the Bills got the ball, Buffalo quarterback Jim Kelly threw an interception. Eight plays later, Emmitt Smith rumbled into the end zone from the 1-yard line to put the Cowboys ahead 27–13. A few moments later, kicker Eddie Murray booted a field goal. Dallas won, 30–13. For the second year in a row, they were Super Bowl champs.

Moments after the game ended, Emmitt learned that on the basis of his 132 rushing yards and two touchdowns, he had been selected Super Bowl MVP, becoming the first player ever to win the rushing title, regular season MVP, and Super Bowl MVP in the same year.

He had achieved all his goals. Now the only question that remained for him was, What do I want to achieve next?

Chapter Ten:
1994-95

Setback

In the off-season, Emmitt Smith had surgery on his damaged shoulder. The doctors discovered that he was injured even more badly than they thought. His collarbone was no longer attached to his shoulder and had to be stabilized. The procedure went well, and he began to look forward to the 1994 season.

Like many other Cowboys, he was shocked when he learned that Dallas coach Jimmy Johnson had resigned. Smith liked Johnson and thought the coach was responsible for much of the team's success.

But Johnson and Dallas owner Jerry Jones had quarreled. Jones believed that anyone could coach the Cowboys to the Super Bowl and had told the press just that. Johnson was offended by the statement and decided to give Jones the opportunity to find out whether he was right.

So Jones hired former University of Oklahoma coach Barry Switzer to take Johnson's place. While Emmitt missed Johnson, he promised himself to play as well as he could for Coach Switzer.

He did, however, decide to make a few changes in his personal life. His big season and MVP trophies made him one of the best-known and most respected players in football. He wrote his autobiography, *The Emmitt Zone*, and began working as a spokesperson for several companies.

He also decided to expand his business interests. Emmitt Smith had learned more about the business world and, although he wanted to play another six or seven seasons, was beginning to think about life after football. Emmitt Incorporated branched out into marketing and promotions, and he formed a second firm, The Emmitt Zone, to handle the licensing of products using his name. He began looking into other businesses as well.

Even though he employs his own family, in the off-season Emmitt Smith plays an active role in his businesses. He helps negotiate his own contracts, and callers to his companies are often surprised when Emmitt answers his own phone.

The off-season also provides him with the opportunity to work with Emmitt Smith Charities, his own nonprofit foundation. The foundation provides support to more than a dozen organizations, from the Salvation Army to the Boys Club and a youth theater group. Every summer, he sponsors a charity golf tournament and an off-season football clinic that fund scholarship programs.

As if that weren't enough, each spring and summer, he also kept making progress on the promise he made to his mother not to build a house until he graduated from college. Every off-season, Emmitt returned to school and kept working toward his degree. By 1994, he was only eighteen credits short of graduation and decided to accelerate his education. He was tired of living in apartments. He wanted to build his own house!

With such a busy schedule, training camp is almost a relief. And once the 1994 season began, he discovered that very little had changed for the Cowboys. The Cowboys' offense was almost identical to the one installed by Jimmy Johnson. After all, Coach Switzer still had Troy Aikman at quarterback, Michael Irvin at wide receiver, and, most important,

Emmitt Smith in the backfield. The Cowboys were expected to make another run at the Super Bowl.

Emmitt Smith started the season with a bang. In the first game of the year, at Pittsburgh, he pounded the Steelers for 170 rushing yards as Dallas won, 26–9. It looked as if the Cowboys were on their way to another Super Bowl.

But after opening the season with two wins, the Cowboys lost to the Detroit Lions, despite 149 yards rushing by Emmitt. Meanwhile, both the Giants and Eagles were playing well.

Fortunately for Dallas, both teams slumped badly in midseason. The Cowboys' defense came through with the best performance in the league, and Dallas took control of the division.

But at the very end of the season, it was Dallas that stumbled. With several players out with injuries, they lost to Cleveland in Week Fourteen, 19–14. Although they defeated New Orleans one week later, in the third quarter Emmitt Smith went down with a badly pulled hamstring muscle in his leg.

The hamstring is the muscle that runs down the back of the thigh. A pulled hamstring muscle is extremely painful and usually slow to heal. Unless it is completely healed, it is easy to re-injure, often worse than before.

The Cowboys were cautious. They wanted Emmitt Smith to be healthy for the playoffs. Although he wanted to play, the team held him out of the last game. For the first time in his professional career, he missed a game because of an injury.

The Cowboys needed him. They scored only ten points in the season finale, and the Giants won, 15–10. Entering the playoffs, the powerful Cowboys had lost two of three and were suddenly struggling.

Yet their 12–4 record was still good enough to earn a bye in the first round of the playoffs. The Green Bay Packers beat Detroit, 16–12, to earn the right to play the Cowboys.

Emmitt's hamstring was still sore. But Dallas couldn't afford to have him sit out. After all, if the Cowboys lost to the Packers, their season was over. The team trainers wrapped his thigh with tape to give him support and hoped for the best.

When the game began, Emmitt Smith was unsure how long he would be able to play. With each step, he felt a sharp tug on the back of his thigh.

But Emmitt Smith set the tone for the game. In

the first quarter, he ran the ball on nearly every play, and Dallas drove down the field. He finally barged into the end zone from the 5-yard line to give Dallas a 7–0 lead.

Green Bay followed with a field goal, then kicked off deep. Dallas took over on its own 6.

The Packers remembered the Cowboys' opening series. They expected to see Emmitt Smith running the football.

That's just what Dallas hoped. Because when Troy Aikman faded back to pass, he saw the Packers' secondary playing tight in anticipation of the run. He then lofted a perfect pass to receiver Alvin Harper streaking downfield. He caught the ball over his shoulder and raced to a 94-yard touchdown — 14–3, Dallas.

The next time the Cowboys got the ball, Emmitt Smith re-injured his hamstring. But by that time, the damage was done. The Cowboys' ground game was well established and Aikman was picking the Packers apart.

Dallas rolled to a big 35–9 win, setting up yet another showdown with San Francisco.

But the Cowboys were concerned about Emmitt

Smith. As they feared, this hamstring pull was worse than the original injury suffered weeks before.

The doctors did what they could to help Emmitt heal. After applying ice for twenty-four hours, they attached electrodes to a battery pack that sent a small current into the thigh. They hoped the current would increase blood flow and speed the healing process.

As the Cowboys practiced, Emmitt rested his leg. The game was scheduled to be played in San Francisco, where a week of rain had turned the field into quicksand.

That was good news for Emmitt Smith. "I'm a pretty good mudder," he told the press. "I'll be out there." He expected to play. That was his goal.

Still, most observers were surprised to see Emmitt Smith take the field against the 49ers, his thigh heavily taped. You just weren't supposed to heal that quickly from a hamstring injury.

The Cowboys knew he wasn't 100 percent. Perhaps that's why they began the game looking to pass the ball.

After receiving the opening kickoff, the Cowboys immediately went to the air. On only the third play of the game, Troy Aikman threw a pass downfield intended for receiver Kevin Williams.

The 49ers' cornerback Eric Davis cut in front of Williams and raced 44 yards for a touchdown. Dallas trailed, 7–0.

Once again, Dallas took the kickoff and tried to move the ball downfield. This time, Michael Irvin fumbled. San Francisco recovered the ball and quickly scored to go ahead by two touchdowns.

For the third time in less than five minutes, the Cowboys received the kickoff. Things went from bad to worse. Kevin Williams fumbled the return; San Francisco scored again to lead 21–0 midway through the first quarter.

The Cowboys didn't give up. They closed the gap to 24–14 on a touchdown pass to Michael Irvin and a 4-yard run by Emmitt Smith before San Francisco quarterback Steve Young threw a touchdown pass to receiver Jerry Rice on the final play of the first half. The game was all but over.

Emmitt contributed a third-quarter touchdown, then pulled the hamstring yet again and was forced from the game. San Francisco won, 38–28. For the first time in three seasons, Emmitt Smith and the Cowboys would not be at the Super Bowl.

While at home resting his hamstring, Emmitt tried to watch the game. "I couldn't stand it," he told a reporter later. "I watched only the first two or three plays and I turned the television off. I knew we should have been there a third time." His goal had been to play in the game, not to watch it on television. And if he couldn't play, he simply wasn't interested.

His off-season was busier than ever. The injury to his hamstring had disturbed him. As he told one writer, "I honestly believe if a healthy Emmitt Smith had played against San Francisco last season, it would've been a different ball game." He worked out harder than ever, focusing on strengthening his leg so the hamstring wouldn't be a problem during the 1995 season.

Then, after spending several hours a day at the gym, he went to school. In a rush to get his degree, he took a full-time course load of fifteen credits. He also opened a new business, Emmitt Smith Communications, that sold phone cards, cellular phones, and beepers, and he began construction of his new house near Dallas.

That didn't mean he had forgotten his promise to his mother. As he explained to a reporter, "My original promise was to get my education before I built the house. As it turns out, I'll have the house before I actually graduate, but I'll be done with my course work." All he needed to do for his degree in health and resort management was to complete an internship.

Emmitt Smith managed his own health extremely well during the off-season and came to training camp in late July in the best shape of his career. He and his teammates knew they had something to prove.

They made that clear to the rest of the NFL in the very first game of the season, on a Monday night against the New York Giants. Dallas took the opening kickoff and returned the ball to its own 25-yard line.

On the first play, Aikman threw to Jay Novacek for 15 yards. Then he threw an incomplete pass. It was now second down and 10. Although this was normally a passing situation, the Cowboys decided to give the ball to Emmitt for his first carry of the season.

He burst through the middle like he was shot from a cannon, knocking over one potential tackler and faking out another. Suddenly, he was all alone. Sixty yards later, he scored.

The run set the tone for the game, and for the season. The Cowboys' defense shut out the Giants, while the offense made use of Emmitt Smith to control the football. He scored three more touchdowns and finished with 163 rushing yards as the Cowboys won, 35–0.

Dallas opened the season with a perfect 4–0 record as Emmitt rushed for more than 100 yards in each game. In Week Five, the Cowboys finally lost to Washington, 27–23, as Emmitt Smith was held to only 95 yards.

But the Cowboys rebounded against Green Bay, winning 34–24, as Emmitt again broke the 100-yard barrier. All his hard work in the off-season was paying dividends. He was off to the best start of his career. Not only was he gaining a lot of yardage, but he was breaking loose for long runs and scoring touchdowns like never before.

The Cowboys opened up a big lead in the Eastern Division. But a midseason 38–20 loss to archrival San

Francisco and losses to Washington and Philadelphia a few weeks later had people questioning whether the Cowboys were prepared for the playoffs.

Suddenly, there appeared to be problems everywhere. Quarterback Troy Aikman was playing on two wobbly knees, the defense had turned soft, and the offensive line wasn't dominating the line of scrimmage. Even Emmitt Smith had slowed down. In the twelfth game of the year, against Kansas City, he sprained his knee. He failed to reach 100 yards in that game, and in two of the next four.

Still, he finished the regular season with 1,773 yards rushing, 25 touchdowns, and 62 pass receptions, all career highs. Yet Emmitt Smith and the Cowboys entered the playoffs surrounded by questions. Were they ready?

With a 12–4 record, the Cowboys had earned a bye during the first week of postseason play. The Philadelphia Eagles obliterated the Detroit Lions in the NFC wild card game, 58–37, and earned the right to play the Cowboys in Dallas.

The Cowboys knew the Eagles would give them a tough game. The two teams had split their two regular-season meetings, and Dallas knew the Eagles would be confident after their big win against Detroit.

Once the game began, the Dallas defense made an early statement, forcing the Eagles to punt on their first three possessions. That gave the Dallas offense a chance to get on track.

In the second quarter, Deion Sanders scored the first touchdown of the game on a 21-yard reverse, and Emmitt Smith followed with a touchdown of his own to put the Cowboys ahead, 17–3, at the half.

They went on to a 30–11 win. Emmitt Smith rushed for 99 yards, Troy Aikman threw for 253, and the Dallas defense dominated. Suddenly, the Cowboys looked like a Super Bowl team!

This time the upstart Green Bay Packers dumped the 49ers in their divisional playoff, leading to a showdown with Dallas for the conference title. The two clubs squared off on January 14, 1996, in Dallas to decide who would go to the Super Bowl.

The Packers proved to be the Cowboys' toughest opponent to date. Packer quarterback Bret Favre directed Green Bay's powerful offense to perfection, leading the Pack to 17 first-half points.

But the Cowboys' offense showed its strength,

too. They responded with 24 points on two Troy Aikman–to–Michael Irvin touchdown passes, a field goal, and a 1-yard plunge by Emmitt Smith.

Yet in the third quarter, Green Bay took command, scoring 10 unanswered points as the Packers' defense shut out Dallas. The Cowboys had fifteen minutes to find a way to win.

They didn't panic. Dallas calmly drove down the field, mixing runs and passes, to the Green Bay 6. Then the Cowboys turned the ball over to Emmitt Smith.

The Packers were expecting a pass. Instead, the Cowboys ran a draw play to the left.

The Cowboys' huge tackle, Nate Newton, blocked two men on the play and opened up a big hole. Emmitt danced through, and the Cowboys regained the lead, 31–27.

Now the defense had to stop Green Bay. They did, intercepting a Favre pass and returning it to midfield.

The Packers expected Dallas to give the ball to Emmitt Smith and try to run out the clock. But the Cowboys crossed them up again as Aikman threw far downfield to Irvin, who made it to the Green Bay 17-yard line.

Now the Packers were expecting another pass. They got Emmitt Smith.

Another draw play to the left worked to perfection. Emmitt raced all 17 yards into the end zone for his 150th rushing yard and third touchdown of the day. Dallas won, 38–27. The Cowboys were going back to the Super Bowl!

Chapter Eleven:
1995–96

Reaching the Goal

This time the Cowboys faced the Pittsburgh Steelers. After starting the season 4–4, Pittsburgh had won seven of its last eight regular-season games, then crushed the Bills and Colts in the playoffs. The Steelers featured a potent offense led by quarterback Neil O'Donnell and triple-threat receiver–running back–quarterback Kordell Stewart and had a big-play defense anchored by linebacker Greg Lloyd.

Entering the game, both clubs wanted to run the football and play ball control. The Steelers knew that the longer they kept the Cowboys' offense — and Emmitt Smith — off the field, the better chance they had to win.

But the Cowboys took the opening kickoff and sent the Steelers a message. They quickly drove to midfield and gave the ball to Emmitt.

The Cowboys ran a trap play, on which the offensive line allows a defensive player to penetrate the line of scrimmage. Then a lineman pulls and blocks the player from the side. If the play works, it usually opens a large hole.

The Steelers' aggressive linebacker Greg Lloyd was the object of the trap. He blasted through the line of scrimmage as Emmitt Smith took the handoff and followed guard Larry Allen. Allen knocked Lloyd to the side, and Emmitt cut through the hole. He ripped off 23 yards before being tackled at the Steeler 28-yard line.

Then the Pittsburgh defense stiffened. Dallas kicker Chris Boniol booted a field goal to put the Cowboys ahead.

Pittsburgh got the ball back but was soon forced to punt. Dallas took over and again drove down the field.

At the Pittsburgh 10-yard line, Dallas ran a play-action pass. Troy Aikman faked the ball to Emmitt Smith, who ran into the line as if he had the ball. The Steelers' linebackers hesitated. By the time they figured out that Aikman still had the ball, tight end Jay Novacek had slipped behind them into the end zone. Aikman threw a perfect pass and now Dallas led, 10–0.

In the second quarter, Boniol kicked another field goal to make the score 13–0. The Steelers were in danger of getting blown out.

But they didn't quit. Just before the half, O'Donnell found receiver Yancey Thigpen in the end zone for a touchdown. The Steelers trailed by six, 13–7.

In the second half, both teams had a chance to move the ball but were forced to punt. When the Steelers got the ball for the second time, they started driving.

On third down and 10 at midfield, Neil O'Donnell dropped back to pass. Under pressure from a blitz, the ball slipped from his hand as he released a pass that floated downfield. Cowboy cornerback Larry Brown intercepted the ball at his own 38-yard line and returned it all the way to the Pittsburgh 19.

The Cowboys didn't waste time. Another play-action pass, this time to Irvin, moved the ball to the 2. Then it was Emmitt Smith's turn.

He took the handoff and charged right up the back of Cowboy guard Larry Allen. He was met at the line of scrimmage by Pittsburgh defensive back Carnell Lake and linebacker Jason Gildon.

For a moment, his forward progress stopped. But he kept driving with his legs, lifting his knees like pistons in an engine.

All of a sudden, he spun free, legs still churning, and tumbled backward into the end zone. Touchdown, Dallas!

Down 20–7, it would have been easy for the Steelers to quit. But they had come too far to give up.

They fought back in the fourth quarter to score ten unanswered points and close to within three, 20–17.

With five minutes left to play, Pittsburgh took over at its own 36-yard line. A Super Bowl win was only 64 yards away. The Dallas defense dug in.

After throwing an incomplete pass, O'Donnell dropped back again on second down. His main receivers were covered, so he looked to receiver Cory Holliday in the right flat and threw the ball.

Larry Brown anticipated the pass. As soon as he saw O'Donnell look to the right side, he started streaking in. He picked off the pass and ran it all the way to the Steeler 6-yard line.

Pittsburgh knew what was coming next but was

powerless to stop it. First, Emmitt Smith carried the ball up the middle for a 2-yard gain. Then the Cowboys ran a "Power Right."

Emmitt took the ball and followed Moose Johnston to the right. Linemen Larry Allen and Erik Williams double-teamed Steeler lineman Brenton Buckner as tight end Jay Novacek sealed off linebacker Kevin Greene. Johnson saw cornerback Myron Bell closing the hole and flattened him.

There were two players left to beat. Emmitt Smith faked past linebacker Levon Kirkland, then took aim at linebacker Chad Brown. Brown was all that stood between Emmitt and his goal.

Running at full speed, Smith charged directly into the linebacker, knocking him backward and tumbling forward. When he hit the ground, he looked down and saw the end zone. He had reached his goal.

The Cowboys won, 27–17. For the third time in four seasons, they were Super Bowl champions!

Larry Brown was selected Super Bowl MVP. The Steelers actually held Emmitt Smith to only 49 yards, his lowest rushing total all year. But they had failed to stop him when they really needed to.

That made him very, very happy. With his goal of

winning a third Super Bowl accomplished, he turned his attention to other matters.

As he had promised his mother, he completed his internship and qualified for his degree. In early May, he invited his entire family to the graduation ceremony at the University of Florida.

Dressed in a black cap and gown, Emmitt looked just like any other student. But when they announced his name, Emmitt J. Smith, the entire University of Florida class of 1996 stood up and applauded its most famous classmate, a sound Emmitt found as sweet as any he had ever heard in a football stadium.

Then, while he shook hands with the university president and took his diploma, a tear came to his eyes as he searched for his mother in the crowd of spectators.

She was easy to find. Mary Smith was waving a huge sign that read PROUD MOM.

After the ceremony, Emmitt found it difficult to contain his emotions. Even after three rushing titles, three Super Bowl championships, and an MVP award, getting his college degree was something special.

"It's one thing to be accepted for your athletic ability," he said. "It's another thing to be standing in an academic arena, to walk across the stage and be recognized for your academic accomplishment. It was special to hear that cheer.

"I'm just as thrilled about this accomplishment as I am about any other accomplishment I have achieved over the past six years," he added.

Coming from Emmitt Smith, the best running back in pro football, that means something.